Beneath The Ashes

The Redemption Arc

N.S. Jangle

India | USA | UK

Made with ❤ on the BookLeaf Publishing Platform
www.bookleafpub.in
www.bookleafpub.com

Dedication

To the kindred spirit holding this book,

In moments of despair, it is often said,
No advice ever beats the comfort of a friend.
I dedicate this collection to those broken and torn,
Searching in the darkness for a familiar soul.

To turn the voices inside out,
We will sing together and beat the doubt.
A song of poems, from dark to bright,
Together, we shall conquer the forever night.

For in the words, we find our place,
A shared journey, a growing space.
Through every tear, through every fight,
We'll rise again and reach out to the light.

From,
N.S. Jangle

Preface

In this raw and unfiltered collection of poems, I invite you to journey through the night—a night that is as much about internal darkness as it is about the search for light. Through these verses, I hope to connect with your own story and offer you a sense of comfort amidst the chaos.

The poems are carefully arranged to follow a progression: *Fall, Conflict, Reflection, Struggle,* and *Confrontation.* Each section is intricately woven into the next, creating a seamless experience for the reader. Their significance has been kept hidden within the pages, but as you continue on this journey, their presence will resonate, unfolding with each turn.

I offer these words to you with the hope that they speak to your heart, reflect your own experiences, and guide you towards redemption.

Yours faithfully,
N.S. Jangle

Acknowledgements

I would like to express my heartfelt gratitude to libraries, both physical and digital, around the world for being open and welcoming sanctuaries of knowledge for all. Their vast collections and endless resources have been a constant source of inspiration.

The influence of poets whose works I have deeply admired and connected with—such as Emily Dickinson, Robert Frost, and Edgar Allan Poe—can be seen throughout my own works. Their words have shaped my voice, and their artistry has guided me on this poetic journey.

Charged on at my flanks

Overhead, an endless sheet of white sea spread,
Beneath me, an ocean - the City, widespread.
Heightened senses made my mind go blank;
I was being charged on at my flanks.

The seventh floor of heaven was my honoured seat,
I slowly inched toward my impending defeat.
My ignorant confidant planned a lively fiesta;
I smiled weakly, not wanting to dim her divine vesta.

Fake smiles devoured my spirit from within,
Dreams turned toxic, knowing there was no win.
Once again, heightened senses made me go blank;
I was being charged on at my flanks.

The throne was no longer content with its king,
And my face disappeared from the world's string.
My body ached, and my mind deteriorated,
I was war-torn, bruised, and defeated.

Black Hope

In the middle of winter,
The ghostly cold turned sinister.
Vast expanses of concrete beneath the sun,
A playground where games are played, where I have
fun.

But over the horizon,
now I see,
A pack of ravens,
flying toward me.

Desolate, I ready my plea -
I desperately yearn for company.
"Look here!" my screams become a trope;
My faith in them was a ravenous, black hope.

The freakish flock flew over me,
And sullied my song, my only remaining wrong.
I fire up the screen and drown in its melody,
The truth gnawing away at my sanity.

Forgotten again;
again, moot -
My life clocked down,
in an endless loop.

Endless Void

Into the abyss I gaze,
No sound, no light,
Nothing ever returns once sent,
Into the abyss I gaze.

Thoughts of improvement,
Too heavy now to implement,
Are cast away into the dark,
Into the abyss I gaze.

It forms a little black hole in my mind,
A garbage disposal I call a shelf.
Thoughts, feelings, memories alike,
Fall endlessly, into the abyss I gaze.

A quiet whirlpool churns within,
As the pieces of me fade and blend,
Each fragment swallowed, lost in time,
Into the abyss, where none ascend.

Yet still I stare, without a choice,
Caught in the silence, in the void's voice,
For though it takes, it never gives,
Into the abyss, I gaze - and live.

The Maze of Mind

Never had his mind worked so hard,
Thoughts so clear, ideas so sharp,
Yet no way forward through the maze of his mind,
A labyrinth he'd built, forgotten with time.

His mind raced fast, but his body stood still,
Frozen in place, a prisoner of will.
Each day it echoed the same tired song,
Fighting the same battles, playing along.

Thoughts like a river, endless and deep,
But in the currents, no answers to keep.
He searched for the path, but the maze had no end,
Trapped in a cycle he couldn't transcend.

No matter the effort, no matter the strain,
The walls of his mind were unyielding, insane.
Every day felt like a mirror of the last,
Repeating the same scars from his past.

He longed for escape, for the maze to unwind,
For the chains of his thoughts to be broken, defined.
But each time he tried, the path blurred and swayed,
And the clarity he craved seemed forever delayed.

In his heart, he knew there was more to be found,
A way to break free, a way to rebound.
But the harder he searched, the less he could see,
A mind so vast, yet locked in its plea.

So he stood in the maze, a captive of thought,
Wishing for the answers he desperately sought.

In my sorrows, I drown

Sometimes, in my sorrows, I drown.
So deep, so down.
My mind becomes my worst adversary,
Memories so sweet, that I crumble underneath.

Like grains of wheat, they slip through my fingers;
Even in my darkest moments, their sweet aftertaste
lingers.
Can I call upon the ghosts of my past?
To relive their glory, their past.

Am I to scramble in the wastelands alone?
Begotten a demon that names me "Lone"?
Crushed in my search for redemption,
I close my bank of thought.

Any embers of hope left are gone,
And my life now falls apart.

The Lost Paw

A hurt cat was hidden in the wild,
No one could find him, not day nor night.
Scared and alone, he had wandered away,
Lost in the shadows, too frightened to stay.

The fearful cat, so distant, so far,
Had slipped from his home, beneath the stars.
In his solitude, he feared to explain,
The pain he carried, the deep, silent strain.

The tired cat, so hungry, so worn,
Searched for food, for water, for warmth.
Through days of struggle, in silence he'd roam,
A world of hardship had become his home.

Nostalgic, he'd dream of his owners' embrace,
But guilt held him captive, time slowed his pace.
He'd caused them so much, his absence too great,
His heart ached with fear, maybe it was too late.

The days stretched on, too many to count,
The time for return seemed to lose all amount.
The cat now feared, with each passing dawn,
That his friends were lost, a chance for return long gone.

A sunny day

Today at the beach, the winds danced away
Turning my pages as I tried to play,
A needed respite from the daily war,
even the heavens wanted to play me a song.

Birds descended from their celestial flight,
Hopping on the damp, green grass so bright.
The sun shone with a silent, aching cry,
And even angels paused, suspended in the sky.

Peace arrived in waves, a boatload to spare,
Ships sailed slowly in the distant air.
but this moment was ephemeral, like a mayfly's day
and this was the only certain, the only way.

Still, I remember that broken star,
Seen through the jungle's twisted bark,
Its warmth greater than any ray I've known,
A fleeting light, a nostalgic home.

The Kings Decree

The king's decree, so firm, so cold,
"No reprieve," his voice was bold.
A future lost, the cost too steep,
A battle-worn, the knight too weak.

He turned away, too tired to fight,
A knight who knew he could not win tonight.
The weight of silence filled the air,
With every step, a prayer, a prayer.

Home awaited, warm and bright,
But his soul had long given up the fight.
The smile he gave, the words he spoke,
A mask to hide the heart that broke.

At the table, laughter filled the room,
But in his chest, there bloomed a doom.
He hid the storm, he wore the guise,
While something inside him said goodbye.

No one knew, not one could tell,
The weight of the king's final spell.
He laughed and nodded, just as before,
While inside, he closed another door.

One Step

One step away now,
Lies the abominable way.
It'll end my everlasting suffering today.
Let the Bells ring away.

One step away still.
I conflict with my choice,
The beauty, the noise.
It sinks me in its eternal voice.

Half a step away now, it is the end.
My heart lost its way,
And the brain finally lost its sway.
It's in motion, it's set, they say.
it doesn't matter now either way.

No step's left to take
Please tell me, Am I dead?
I can still feel the pain. In my chest, my neck.
Let's try again tomorrow, alive to die on another deck.

Beauty turns Putrid

As I walk down the picturesque street,
Surrounded by the beauty of every being,
All I can see are things out of reach —
Every beauty turns putrid within me.

A switch is flipped deep in the brain,
When happiness breeds envy, and joy feels vain.
Every pretty thing that once sparked delight
Now brings only dread, replacing light.

When every other soul seems to find
The dreams you've longed for, now intertwined,
And the world around you is vibrant, bright —
But you're trapped in shadows, devoid of light.

They wear the colours of success and grace,
While you're the only one left in a grayscale place.
A painted world, but you can't fit in,
Forever seeking beauty, but finding sin.

Doctrine of Living

Death is sweet, and death is bitter,
Sweet to us, but bitter to others.
Death, the place where we count no more,
Where the heart's burdens cease to pour.

Life is bitter, yet life is worth,
A struggle that shapes us, gives us birth.
Life, though bitter, leaves us a trace,
A legacy we pass through time and space.

Rebirth is sweet, rebirth brings light,
Hope is born in the darkest night.
In belief, we find a new way to cope,
Rebirth weaves together bitter and hope.

The Chains of Intellect

It would be easier still,
If I were a brat, a dill,
To have fallen so low,
A sore sight to my own soul.

If I were just an average Joe,
Perhaps this pain would never show.
Setbacks would be the norm,
And I'd live my life in endless storms.

But my mind, sharp yet cruel,
Gave me a fate that felt so cruel—
Not at the hand of Jill or Dave,
But by my own hand, I was enslaved.

My thoughts, my doubts, my constant fight,
Led me to question even the right.
Where others find a simple grace,
I stumble in this endless race.

For intellect is a double-edged sword,
That cuts deeper than I can afford.
It makes me see the flaws I hide,
And leaves my heart broken inside.

It sets the bar too high for me,
Demands perfection constantly.
Where others bend and bounce back fast,
I break at setbacks, caught in the past.

Now that I've destroyed all I've built,
My mind just twists the threads of guilt—
Instead of seeing the foolish choice,
I intellectualize, give it a voice.

Analyzing every move I made,
When all I should do is let it fade.
I can't just fail and simply try,
I've built a prison where I can't fly.

Lies I tell

There are these lies I tell,
Sabotaged you & I as we fell,
Bad as I felt about them,
I turned again, to my old friend.

Habit covered for me with excuses,
Weakness served me reasons.
My facade blasted into smithereens,
Call out again, to my dear old friend.

Lies as they are,
Are harmless like ham,
Till you dig up their origins,
And find pig remains.

I wallowed in my despair,
Playing the victim to my crimes.
Who else can cover for me now?
When I am no longer there. Old friend.

Mask

I wear a mask, a perfect disguise,
To hide the tempest behind my eyes.
Beneath it, chaos brews and tears,
But all you see are smiles and cheers.

The burden of the truth, a heavy weight,
I carry it, though it's too late.
The mask cracks, but not too wide,
For fear of what will run inside.

Am I still the same if they knew it all?
Or will the weight of truth make me fall?

Ocean's Shore

Tied to a post on the ocean's shore,
Tomorrow is a myth, a lore
But first, today we must survive,
To make it through the fall of night.

Wave after wave, we must uphold,
Our tired souls, our tortured throne.
Even after the cruellest fight,
Tomorrow will reignite the plight.

It's not pain, nor sorrow's face,
But the endless tide, the endless days.
Nothing new, no change in sight,
Just drifting in the monotony of night.

It could've been years, or mere hours passed,
Since I was bound to this mast,
All I feel are waves crashing in,
Yet even that has lost its sting within.

Through the Glass Wall

Through the glass walls, I could see,
The victims of my deception smiling at me.
Honesty would have shattered my mask,
And pretence, I couldn't have made it last.

I thanked the glass walls in between,
For protecting them from what I'd been.
To help them see elsewhere,
And obscure the teary streams I bear.

With every interaction, I was forced to lie,
Pushing the last of them away, just to let them smile.
With a delusional hope I might solve it all,
And if not, never let the pain reach these halls.

These glass walls were my castle once,
Many castles have I lost.
But I will always thank these glass walls,
For glass walls were all I watched.

Plan for Doom

I thought a lot back in those days,
Of what I would do, what I would say.
Not to face my fears and foes,
But to give justifications to friends and shows.

Paralyzed by doubt, I stood still,
Laying down my arms, against my will.
Long before the war's loud call,
I'd already set myself to fall.

Had I planned for success, maybe it might've worked,
But the fear I carried in me only lurked.
Rational thoughts felt far away,
As my ideas crumbled, led astray.

The weight of weakness, too much to bear,
Made my plans fall apart in mid-air.
What I feared most was never the fight,
But the doom I created in my own mind's sight.

Prisoner

Today I sat with my captor,
Looked him straight in the eyes.
Asked him his reason,
For binding me in this disguise.

He stared back, sorrowful,
Seeing me so weak,
Though in this cell we share,
Only silence dares to speak.

Guard and prisoner,
We counted the days,
Ticking down to the verdict,
The one we had both made.

I asked him, "Why do you stay,
And keep me locked within?
I built these walls myself,
And you are just my sin."

He whispered, "You're the key,
The lock and the chain,
The one who holds the power,
Yet you remain in pain."

19. The Lost Crown

Before the fall had come the prime
And it made everything hurt to a nine
One it left behind for diabolical hope
It felt like a bad episode of a soap

My story was glorious and filled with tales
Of conquests and defeats of fabled days
And this campaign was to be the crowning jewel
Like Napolean and Moscow, I got reduced too

Tomorrow again I'd return to the original shine
I waited and waited, to wake up I pine
May this be a dream, a song, a sham
I prayed, I prayed, but my prayers hit a dam

Distorted reality and realistic delusions,
the war waged on within my mind
Too tired and weary had become the knight
To fight the battles outward and stand in the light.

The crown had flown away in a flood,
Only survival now remained.
Riches were now a far gone goal
Every drop of blood I now looked to save.

Skyline that could have been

Looking out the windowed wall,
I see the skyline, once adored,
A vision of what could have been,
Now fading, slipping through my hands.

A stellar record of battles won,
Would echo in the songs unsung,
My life, a beacon bright and bold,
A tale for every soul to hold.

The glass and steel beneath me rise,
But now they only cloud my eyes.
What once was mine, my kingdom grand,
Now slips like sand through grasping hands.

The skyline shifts, its glory fades,
What once was promised now evades.
Yet still, I stare, and in the haze,
I chase the dream of brighter days.

The Fall

It was a spring when it all went wrong,
For no good reason to write a song.
One by one, things fell apart,
And pieces of me started to depart.

It wasn't a sign of stupidity,
I had seen superior people pass.
Neither was it ambition,
I was running after the stars.

I often wondered what I would say
When people would eventually ask,
Of ways to save myself the trouble,
Till even that came to a stop.

Now I chase after the ghosts
Of my fallen dreams and thoughts,
Never to measure up again
To my platinum future, of the past.

Lazy Warrior

Once upon a time, a warrior so bold,
Whose ambition burned bright, his story was told.
He swore to the heavens, to the stars he would rise,
Yet never once trained under earthly skies.

With a heart full of fire, he dreamed of the fight,
Of conquering realms, of wielding his might.
In his hometown, he was the best by far,
Crowned in glory, a local shining star.

But when he met knights of true valor and skill,
His confidence faltered, his dreams turned still.
For though he was praised by those unaware,
Against seasoned warriors, his talent was rare.

Hypocrisy reared its ugly face,
As the warrior realized his slow pace.
He had spoken of greatness, of battles to win,
But lacked the discipline that true strength begins.

Yet, despite the truth, despite the shame,
The warrior continued to play the same game.
He spoke of his victories, his sword's mighty swing,
But still, in his heart, no real training would bring.

For dreams are sweet, but effort is key,
And ambition alone cannot set you free.
The warrior, though lazy, still thought he'd prevail,
But without the work, his dream would fail.

In the end, he learned the hardest of truths,
That glory demands the sweat of the youth.
For the stars may beckon, the skies may call,
But without practice, no one will stand tall.

Obsessions and Compulsions

Somewhere shallow obsessions are born,
By the time you reason, the reason is gone.
All that's left is a limitless void,
That you must try to fill with a silent voice.

Obsessions are not fun or folly,
They are a part of what makes you rally.
They laser your focus from your limitless ways,
Either drive you up or dig your grave.

They aren't singular in nature,
Nature isn't ever that neat.
You have multiple obsessions fighting,
Fighting amongst themselves to feed your needs.

Compulsions are what we see,
They are the actions that quell our need.
Slaves to the obsessions we seed,
But flak is never born by the desire, but the deed.

Controlling compulsions brings clarity,
To think such a falsehood is a dastard parody.
To clear your compulsions is a daily death,
The death of the obsessions that you set.

Fact and Fiction

Fact and fiction start to mingle,
Somewhere deep, thoughts begin to linger.
Lingering thoughts replace the past,
Memories altered, forever cast.

When every person is a story retold,
How many new faces can you hold?
Before the weight of memories you feign
Begins to outweigh the comfort they contain?

Lies are a useful tool,
But honesty is far better.
Pain is dealt with once, then thrown,
But pretending lasts forever, till overthrown.

False memories begin to form,
A defence against that needed song -
The song you chose to hide,
Simply because it was an inconvenient tide.

25. Procrastination

Problems are funny that way,
The biggest ones always turn you away.
And you end up working on the ones
Which never held any sway.

Funnier still is the avoidance of them all,
How the brain believes this works—
I shall never understand it at all,
The pile rises while you take a stroll.

For the fear of facing mountains,
Versus the ignorant sleep of the mind,
I cannot fault anyone,
Least myself, as I run away in time.

Soon, I'll figure myself out,
I'll solve this one day.
But that day—today—is not,
And tomorrow, it's still not,
Exactly as I thought.

Burden of Expectations,
People forget how heavy are,
They keep piling them on, and on.

Prolonged Nights

At the last hit of the hour's hand
a rationale starts to build.
To compensate for the pouring hail,
by running in the dark that begins

But the world is tired
And so are we,
Running isn't what we can.

promising ourselves tomorrow's better,
that sounds like a better plan.

Neither fighting, nor do we rest,
we prolong that dastard night.
Delude ourself we might actually work,
when tomorrow is all we prevent

The Enemy

In the grimmest moment, I looked,
At the place, I thought I already took.
Ripped out of my hands again,
It's something I cannot tolerate.

Foolish decisions have gotten me here,
Fooler shall I be,
when I come back with an army,
Not for the gold, but for the queen.

Grief does not process in my head,
Instead, I lash out in a blinded rage.
From the Bestiary I take a page,
Act out in its mirror image.

My fury set my world on fire,
And my rage drowned the survivors.
This humiliation is one I cannot take.
Prepare to have my life staked.

Vengeful is my true nature,
Hidden under a facade of layers.
I maim and torture in my head, my heart,
Till I do it with my hands, my arms.

Scavenge to my core, and I might find some bone.
With a mineral of goodness, stolen from me
Now I am pain-embodied. I ache to my core.
Making me suffer is my only hope.

The Deepening Lull

The deeper we sink,
The deeper we sleep.
Lazy with our time,
Lazy with our rhyme.

Lethargy grips, slow and tight,
Lethargy dims the fading light.
The pieces fall, they drift apart,
But no force stirs to make a start.

We search for reasons, but none are found,
We search for meaning in silent sound.
Trying becomes too much to bear,
Fighting for nothing, nothing to care.

Lethargy breathes, it feeds on itself,
Lethargy thrives in the stillness of health.
We won't rise, we won't fight,
We lie, and we drift, out of sight.

A Treatise on Confidence

Confidence isn't a constant state,
I build it again every day,
Repetition is its fastest friend.
Easily gained,
Easily lost,
It shaves off quicker than it's born.

A lull is its arch-enemy,
It drives it to the ground,
And makes it grow upside down.
Fueled by following your beliefs,
It doesn't accept retreats,
Truly a headfast and stubborn shield.

In moments of desperation, I have called it upon,
Death wish or courage are its forms,
Soon to disappear, they're fast to appear.
An inner voice guides my many actions,
It's the key to get through tough days,
Following it will grant my destiny for every day.

Self-respect is that key's name,
Following it gives me untold strength.
My fears vanish like they were never there.
Hold a mirror to your face and see,
Am I attracted to the person before me?
It's the end all of all our feats.

Confidence grows up like trees,
Watered since it was a sapling.
Loved since 'twas just a seed.
If you don't feel you deserve it,
It is what you most need,
Cry, try, bite, hold on to that.

I see the person before me,
Ashamed is what I feel,
Today is the day of reversing the scales.
Ashamed of me shall everyone be,
And I'll stand tall in my unearned confidence,
With no lies to shelter, smiling back at them.

Survival Mode

Daily chores felt like a mountain's weight,
Sustenance became a constant state.
Thriving was a distant, fleeting dream,
Survival mode was now the theme.

Passing a day felt like a mighty win,
Simply seeing tomorrow was a nightly spin.
When these tasks turned into a constant threat,
There was no room for anything yet.

Like cavemen, I moved without thought,
In the rhythm of struggle, with no rest sought.
Between our minds, no chasm lay,
Just the instinct to survive each day.

After slipping into survival's grip,
There was only lethargy in each slip.
No room for joy, no spark to ignite,
Just the dull rhythm of day into night.

A Ring of the Plastic Box

A ring of that little plastic box
Sends up my spine an irredeemable gasp,
And little tings of its presence
Cast a spell of fear deep in my essence.

The same box is which I escape to now,
When the going starts looking tough.
Mindlessly dazed is what I become,
Its clutches are one I could not overcome.

Numbness or a path to normalcy,
Both could the tiny box have delivered.

But I averted, I averted, I averted,
And I averted, I averted.

The Illusion of Effort

The illusion of effort casts a shadow long,
It feels like progress, though the threat stays strong.
We tackle tasks in the reverse of their need,
Convincing ourselves that we're planting the seed.

Yet the great dangers still lurk in the dark,
Growing bigger, sharper, leaving their mark.
Day after day, the deception persists,
We craft monsters that begin to exist.

We fool our minds into thinking we've grown,
While the real threats continue to be known.
The more we delay, the stronger they grow,
Until we're trapped in a world of our foe.

True Cheer

Not every cheer holds the same power,
And it's not always the caster who must change.
If you've never shown your weakest side,
A true cheer remains untapped, untamed.

If it's been a while since a compliment felt real,
Look inward and ask yourself,
Have you let anyone see your fears,
Or do they cheer for the mask you've made?

A false persona can never hear truth,
For real compliments never reach them.
They praise what's not you, what's not your face,
While your true self stands behind the wall.

Lonely and desolate, you're left to stand,
In the silence where your true self cries.
For only when you drop the mask you wear,
Will true cheer find its way to your life.

The compliments you seek are born in truth,
But they can't reach the version you pretend to be.
And in the quiet of your guarded heart,
You'll find only emptiness where cheer should be.

Permission to be

Is it fair, I ask,
Can I be bad?
Is it important to be,
Always caring for everybody?

How could I be so careless?
Is that your question?
What about the essence of my existence?
I'm still struggling with that direction.

Growth is my prerogative,
Failure a noble task.
I won't settle—
But am I allowed to stumble at last?

Can I be angry?
Can I be selfish?
Can I lash out?
Can I break that glass?

Do I have the right to be silent,
Or still be trusted without a word?
To be quiet for an hour, no questions asked,
And still have you cover my back, undeterred?

Shades of life

Life may seem black or white,
So simple, like day turning night.
But in the shadows, we found our fight,
When we chased dreams with all our might.

There must be moments of flying kites,
Soaring high through peaceful heights,
But winds may change, the storms ignite,
Drizzled in these darkest nights.

Through every fall, there's strength we find,
A spark of hope within the mind.
In every tear, a lesson we sign,
And in the dark, the light intertwines.

So when it feels like you're losing sight,
Remember the sun will rise, so soon, so bright.
Life's not just black, neither is it white,
But a canvas painted in every shade of light.

A Coffee Break

Coffee is great,
A pause, a break,
A chance to see a friendly face.

Coffee is good,
A boost to your day,
A reason to step outside,
And chase the clouds away.

It calls you out,
From the house where you hide,
Into the light,
Away from where you've cried.

So when you say "I feel blue",
Go buy a coffee to share a smile,
At least one face, to break the silence,
Before the night lingers for a while.

37. Obscure our gaze

When looked through the daily gaze,
The goal is obscured always.
So many events occur that smudge the glass,
What was once the aim is now somewhere lost.

We start looking inwards as we grow,
Troubled by our worries, troubled by our woes.
Further pulled away from the fray,
About us, there will be no songs to stay.

For those who run from battles,
For those who couldn't stand,
Let this be a warning:
We won't be a memory when we are sand.

Let this be the last battle you flee,
And if it isn't over, start to run wild and free.
Etch your name in your enemy's heart,
May it be a foe or your own created farce.

Wear your dreams as a tattoo on your heart,
Be full of angst, make full the arc.
Fight for your destiny, to play your part.
Once we are dust, only our legends will last.

Bitter Hill

Nothing is worse
Than being the only bitter one
In a world
Where everyone glitters in the sun.

To sit on a hill
And see what you could have been,
Perhaps another life,
Because this one has come undone.

Pieces have fallen,
The fall will come by the end of the day.
Take everything in,
Because bitter will leave, and the hill will stay.

The next time, we see this place.

Author of Fate

Surrounded by stories, I pen a script,
Of a life desired, one that could be lived.
I became the author of a dystopian art.
To live as the protagonist, not the god.

In moments where my control slips away,
I seize what I can, no matter the price I pay.
Bit by bit, I reclaim the shattered parts,
Every small victory, a return to the start.

If I must fall, I'll name the place,
Choose the hour, design the space.
I'll command the world, and direct the flow,
Plan my doom, yet rise, and grow.

For even in ruin, I am still the pen,
I write my fate, again and again.
Through every collapse, I'll craft anew,
A cycle of death and rebirth, true.

Lion's Den

As I headed into the lion's den,
My death was already written in.
No match for my encroaching fate,
I was destined to soon meet my end.

As I knocked on death's door,
Strange creatures took over my conscious.
Filled me with grief and regret,
Till I cried a teary stream in despair.

The future seemed so bleak,
I thought of cutting short,
the wait the worry,
Instead of watching, it is ended for me.

Brave, I enchanted a spell,
to feel no pain in the lion's den.
Clinging to a fraction of chance,
I charged in legs first, head last.

How my battle will go I cannot tell,
the power of freedom courses through my veins.
In my despondent state,
I unlocked my greatness within.

A promise was made for the enchanted spell,
A life rejected will be lost in a second.
In return for fearless strength,
my mind turned plastic, no bend.

A snap would no longer just stretch,
Once I enter the Lion's Den.

Today Bound

Somewhere far away, there lies a way
To slay every foe and save the day.
But today, alas, I do not hold that sway,
And today is the only time I get to play.

To win an unwinnable battle feels too grey,
Much of myself will rest today,
Buried deep where shadows lay,
In that putrid depth of the ground, I say.

Yet every word will carry its weight,
A single day, a decade's fate.
Such are the days I longed to see,
And when they come, I shall see them, not flee.

Today I Stood Bare

Today I stood bare before my past,
With the eyes of others watching my wrongs.
People who could have made the pain last,
Instead chose to take me in their arms.

A valiant knight, a broken king,
And a saint, heartbroken,
All shaken, they brawled,
All wept in that shared, silent fall.

My pain turned to tears,
My fears went numb.
Nothing had changed,
And everything changed a lot.

Soon I was bare before my foes,
And my friends saw it all.
My family cheered me on,
To be bare was the turnaround after all.

Demons Vanish

Empowered I was,
To feel all the demons vanish.
Putting thoughts to the test of reality,
They soon perished.

Born of my own fears,
They were never mean't to be,
Living among the angels,
Who reside in me.

The love I felt from others,
It gave me a second chance,
To believe in myself enough,
To dance that daring dance.

Now I will run,
not walk.
Fly,
not crawl.

Knowing the despair of hell,
I live on my toes,
inching even a little,
to the heaven's door.

Half-Year of my existence,
For a lifetime of virtue,
I call that a fair trade,
What about you?

Hope and Hopeless

Hope and hopeless shall both meet their demise
In the face of even the smallest misery and strife.

Is it discipline then that rules that fight?
But habit never overcame the brutal might.

Skill neither has protected the pride,
When fear struck, no one took a stride.

Wisdom is also good and well,
But it crumbled when came the knocks on the gates of
hell.

Strength alone has proven itself,
To stand in the face of misery, a brute or plight.

Seek strength then instead of hope,
Character, body, and mind.

Not even the demon will dare to take a stroll,

When strength is in your soul.

65

Carpe Diem x Nightmares

Do nightmares pass?
Do they survive some way?
Lodge themselves in a corner of our mind,
And resurface when the mind is astray?

Are they just dreams we encounter in our sleep?
Or do they include the fearful days?
They make us run down deep,
Till "quiet down" is all we can say.

Nightmares come and go,
Till you forget they stay.
That is how they survive,
Right underneath your gaze.

To pluck them out,
There is only one remedy:
To seize the day
And face the demons that underneath lay.

Postcard

A picture is worth a thousand moments.
Moments it eternalises forever,
Forever, they hold a memory,
A memory of a moment that has passed.

Take back a worthy picture in your parting moments,
Moments you'd like to hold on to forever.
Forever, it will connect you to the memories,
Memories of moments that could have passed.

A picture will take you back to the moments,
Moments you want to visit forever.
Forever, you will live the memory,
Memories that soon will have passed.

Grey Gaze

A piercing grey gaze is what I seek,
A look so sharp, it makes them weak.
Eyes that command, make hearts attend,
And make them listen when I look at them.

Eyes that can pierce the soul within,
Cut through the fog and see beneath the skin.
Though I was not born with such a sight,
Lenses will lend me that inner light.

A steely resolve, reflected clear,
To fix my life and conquer fear.
Grey eyes to see beyond the skies,
To chart my rise, no longer tied.

For though these eyes are not my own,
Through coloured lenses, strength is grown.
They are the shields I wish to wear,
To face the world with a care.

Blemishes and Scars

Like tattoos of victories,
I had blemishes and scars,
Of battles I had lost
At home and afar.

A witch once told me,
Ailments would reflect my soul,
Manifesting in ways, parallel to
The fears that I hold.

No medicine could stop it,
And everyone, I did try—
Healers from around the world
Sighed a silent cry.

Once again, I was reminded
Of the young witch's prophecy:
The recovery of myself,
Externally, wouldn't it come.

Years ahead, I finally learned,
Not by choice, but by burn.
The witch's prophecy did hold true—
The illness faded when my soul came through.

A heart that pains

Before I went through my own little arc,
I was cold and cruel, distant and stark.
To those with hearts broken, torn apart,
I had their respect, but never played the part.

I never understood their silent cry,
I thought they simply hadn't tried.
I judged them from a place of pride,
Blind to the pain they tried to hide.

I mocked the struggles they could not shake,
Unaware of the toll that they did take.
I hated my own stint, a bitter strain,
But from my fall, I became a man again.

Now I carry a heart that pains,
I've learned to walk with open hands.
For through my pain, I found the grace
To see the hurt in another's face.

Beauty in Art

Artists have a flair for the dramatic,
They dramatize every sob,
Laugh in the face of normalcy,
When normalcy is all they ever sought.

In their poems, sometimes you can feel
The rawness of every human cask.
Over caskets of their emotions are built upon,
The roads that will outlast even them.

Poets are by far worse
Than every other craft.
They find solace in misery,
Misery they think will forever cast over them.

Happiness doesn't suit them,
Peace, they can settle for that.
I wonder what's so beautiful to them
About a tired and broken mast.

I have my answer,
This endeavour started from that—
To leave behind a little beauty
In the aftermath of the wreckage that I call the past.